WHERE DO ANGELS GO?

WHERE DO ANGELS GO?

BABY KEEPSAKE IN MEMORIUM

AN AUTOBIOGRAPHICAL SELF-HELP
JOURNAL FOR PARENTS WHO HAVE
EXPERIENCED INFANT LOSS.

Melissa Slaughter-Swingler

iUniverse, Inc.
New York Lincoln Shanghai

Where Do Angels Go?
Baby Keepsake In Memorium

All Rights Reserved © 2003 by Melissa Slaughter-Swingler

iUniverse, Inc.

For information address:
iUniverse, Inc.
2021 Pine Lake Road, Suite 100
Lincoln, NE 68512
www.iuniverse.com

ISBN: 0-595-28915-0

Printed in the United States of America

To my daughter, Angel. She died
On January 17, 1988, before birth,
And was delivered on January 20, 1988, stillborn.

Also to Jacquline-Monique, Baby Kenny,
my brother, Robert, and all the other little angels who
have touched our lives.

Contents

Acknowledgements

Special thanks to:
My Dad (who has passed over),
My Mom, Lisa Uncles, who has become a midwife (fifteen years after Angel's spirit was freed). Mr. Vernon Lake (a great teacher and friend),
Cynthia Gerard, Bridgette Julius-Willaims, Lillian A. Miller, Jean Etsinger, the St Thomas, V.I., Share Support Group, the Cape Cod Chapter of Compassionate Friends, my husband, Frank, and our daughter, Gabrie, and most of all, to God and our Angel.

How to use this book:

This is an autobiographical, self-help journal/workbook. Although physicians, friends, social workers and other family members can use it, its primary use is as a journal/workbook for any woman who experiences the death of an infant, or loss of a young child.

This journal is designed to assist the mother, from acknowledgement of her infant's death, through the course of a year of the grief process.

Personal anecdotes are provided to help the mother recognize stages and symptoms of grief, as well as to facilitate free expression in helping the mother to feel more in control of the situation.

This book is a keepsake that I developed while in the hospital to fill gaps of time between visitors and sleep.

Prologue

Life and death are two sides of the same coin. In the natural order of things, one does not exist without the other. Notwithstanding this, the notion of death is difficult for us to understand and as a result, is a feared state of being. The fear of death contributes to our inability to deal with the death of loved ones as well as our own motility. It is almost impossible for us to imagine not being in the "real" world, not to feel, to see, to love and to be loved. Our inability to cope with this natural progression from birth to death causes us to skirt the issue, to deny the reality or to bury it beneath platitudes. We fail to comfort those suffering a loss because we cannot be comforted in the face of our mortality. Much of this may have to do with our concept of time. Our existence is felt to be temporal/infinite. This view of the world is linear. It begins and ends. The end is only decay. This lends itself to a view of the world that objectifies, and thereby distances us from nature and that which cannot be understood in a physical way.

An Africanized view of the world is circular/cyclical. You know, "What goes around comes around". There are no gaps between self, nature, and super-nature, which are beyond the physical/visible world. There is a unity, a harmony, that promotes and maintains a balance, wholeness in the world (self/internal and universe/external). As a result, in all things there is life. Therefore, one exists alone and as a part of a family, a community, a society, a world and a universe. All things, seen or unseen, are interrelated. Then the concept of time, which is to be experienced, not managed, does not separate past, present and future. They encompass each other. Human life is the same rhythm of nature. Birth (entry into the community of the living) exists on a continuum to death and entry into the community of the departed/dead (ancestors who still live), and finally into the community of the spirits (where all things are one!)

One lives as long as there is one person to remember one's name. Therefore, one is immortal, since one continues to live in the community of the spirits when none are left to remember one's name. The world consists of those who have departed and are remembered (the past, the ancestors), those living in the present, and the not-yet-born, who are the future. Death is a move to anther stage, another aspect of the rhythm in the natural order of things, which is to move to becoming a total person.

There is no end to human history. It continues towards infinity because it is part of the natural rhythm of the universal life cycle, and is therefore renewable.

Therapy is the science of taking care of disease. Psychotherapy is the art of taking care of the psychic pain. In order for the art of psychotherapy to be effective it must be relevant to the experience of the sufferer, the client. It must take the client's assumptions into consideration.

Understanding family dynamics, culture, and the role of religion in the client's reality is an important factor in enabling clients to identify, understand and learn to utilize their internal resources.

Psychotherapy provides tools for understanding one's deficits; recognizing one's resources and using these to find resolution for the Psychic pain that is being experienced, (Psychic pain, unlike physical pain, is very elusive). It demands the willingness of the client to accept difficult work in an effort to heal the heart and the spirit. Psychotherapy's purpose is to seek harmony among the mind, body, and spirit/soul.

When one is in tune with the universe, death is not the end of all things. It is part of life. Death in the natural world begins the process of regeneration.

Energy—the soul, the spirit, which is essence of all being—cannot be destroyed. Why do we then assume that upon the death of a loved one their essence (energy) is as temporal as their body (matter)? If this is not true, then communication between energies is possible. This communication allows for the acceptance of loss and the acceptance of one's reality and to be receptive to all possibilities, natural and super-natural (beyond the natural/matter).

This self-help journal/keepsake is a wonderful way to begin to work through pain, to accept and resolve the death of a loved one—a baby. The death of anyone we love is devastating and unexplainable, but can be rationalized. But the loss of a baby is even less explainable, almost impossible to rationalize. Who is to blame? Initially, the mother usually takes on responsibility for the death of "her baby". Sometimes, "God" is held accountable.

Notwithstanding, the result is depression. Mothers ask the question, why? They receive no answer!

This self-help journal/keepsake can be the beginning, a process that ends in the release of the patient's and infant's energies so that the spirit can rest and the living can get on with living.

Psychotherapist
lillian a miller

"When God Calls Little Children"

When God calls little children
To dwell with him above,
We mortals sometime question
The wisdom of his love.
For no heartache compares with
the death of one small child,
Who does so much to make our world
Seem wonderful and mild.
Perhaps God tires of calling
The aged to his fold,
So He picks a rosebud
Before he can grow old.
God knows how much we need them,
and so he takes but a few,
To make the land of Heaven
More beautiful to view.
Believing this is difficult, still
Somehow we must try,
The saddest word mankind knows will always be "Goodbye."

So when a little child departs
we who are left behind
must realize God loves children,
Angels are hard to find.

Unknown

Hush Little Baby

On the morning of January 17, 1988, at about 3 a.m., I was awaken by a sweet, soft voice. I remember thinking at that moment; "it must be an Angel." Although I was unable to make out the words I was hearing, I felt a peace over and through my entire body. Someone was sitting at the foot of my bed, someone I could not see, a presence I could feel and an inner sense of translucent gray matter.

Getting out of bed, I decided to sit in my rocking chair and stroke my abdomen and sing to my baby, "Hush little baby, don't say a word..." Choking back my tears, I knew I was saying goodbye to my baby, and that my baby was saying goodbye to me.

The words of a Christian song flashed into my mind, and I remembered thinking that it was important that I sing the words of the song. However, I did not know the entire song.

Got any rivers you think are uncrossable? Got any mountains you can't tunnel through? God specializes in things thought impossible;...

After pacing my apartment, squatting, and bathing in warm water, I finally was able to go back to sleep. At 9 a.m. I woke up and called my friend Lisa on the telephone: "Take me to the hospital," I said, "something is wrong."

Empty Arms

"How sweet to hold a newborn baby,
And feel the pride, and joy he gives;
But greater still the calm assurance,
This child can face uncertain days
Because He lives."

—William J Gaither

I was hooked up to the fetal heart monitor, but there was a heart-rending silence, no movement and a single heart-beat—mine. Then a sudden thrust, the last kick, a final reflex.

As I gazed into the grave faces of two doctors who stood over me, I asked, "Is my baby dead?" Finally, one said, "I think so."

On January 20, 1988, three days after my baby's spirit left my body; a baby girl was delivered, stillborn. It seemed that everyone in the delivery room simultaneously gasped, then I heard the nurse say, "She's beautiful." For that second, I was a mother; I was proud.

She was wrapped in a receiving blanket I had brought into the delivery room with me, a blanket I had received at a baby shower, a blanket I had placed in my "hospital Bag" and dreamed of wrapping my infant in, a blanket that would enclose her in my love. Ever so gently, she was placed in my arms.

I don't remember how long I held her, but all too soon my arms were empty. She was taken away forever; my baby was dead. I needed something to hold, for my arms ached. I wanted someone to hold me, but was afraid to ask, afraid I would not be able to let go.

Nothing heals like time; nothing could ever replace Angel. Holding other babies made me realize how empty my arms were, and hugging stuffed animals reminded me how great my loss had been.

Hardest times for me were nights before I fell to sleep, or mornings when the realization of the empty crib, empty womb and empty arms let me know that I wasn't dreaming.

Notes:

Lifetime Memories

Every woman reacts differently to the death of her infant. However, it is certain that all experience shock. It is like a cloud or fog that makes everything seem so unreal. Time for me just slowed down, and each day seemed a weeklong.

I was upset that my daughter was buried only in her sleeper, without a Pamper or a diaper. In the back of my mind I remembered my mother always talking about clean underwear. "No matter what is wrong with you, you must have on clean underwear." I felt that for me, providing an undergarment became synonymous with being a "good" mother.

I had nothing pink for my daughter. She was a girl, and I wanted her to have something pink! I finally decided I would place a pink stuffed animal in her grave.

No one asked if I wanted my baby baptized. Even after the burial it still bothered me. I was given a form to sign in the hospital. My daughter was represented by the word "baby". No one asked me if I wanted to name her. My baby had a name! How could I mourn a person without a name? How could she be a person without a name? How could she live on inside of me if she didn't have a name?

I had such a short time with her, and a lifetime of memories to make. My suggestions to anyone going through a death of this nature:

- Ask to name your child. It's difficult to mourn someone without a name.

- Ask to see your child, to hold your child, to say goodbye. Ask to have pictures taken of your child after he/she has been cleaned up and dressed in an outfit you have chosen. If you're not ready to look at the pictures, ask that they be placed in a sealed envelope (maybe even placed in your hospital records).

- If it's important to you, arrange or have someone arrange a baptism for the child (hospital social workers may be a good resource).

- Ask for a special time to be alone with your child. You need time to see the family resemblance, and the uniqueness of this precious being. You need time to talk to your baby, to hold your baby, to rock him/her in your arms and sing a lullaby (other family members may want to share in this time)

- You may want the baby to be wrapped in a blanket, or want to keep the nametag or items placed on the baby.

- Hospital personnel should treat your infant as other infants are treated—weight, handprints, measurements, and footprints should be recorded for the parent(s).

You should not leave the hospital without important information, such as the names and numbers of therapists in your community who Work with grieving parents, support groups, or hotline numbers that you can call. You should have names of books, articles and other reading materials that are helpful.

- Ask for a lock of your baby's hair (if possible).

This list has been complied from personal experiences, hindsight, and lists found in <u>When Hello Means Goodbye,</u> and an article entitled, "When Things Go wrong.

(List memories that are important to you)

1.

2.

3.

4.

5.

6.

7.

8.

9.

10.

Doctors/Pediatricians

Nurses

Midwives

Hospital Social Workers

Nurses' Aides

Laboratory Technician

Other Support Staff

Visitors

Name   Date

Name   Date

Name   Date

Name   Date

Name   Date

Name   Date

Name   Date

Name   Date

Name   Date

Name   Date

Name   Date

Name   Date

Name   Date

Name   Date

Name   Date

Home-going

Have a part of planning the service for your child; it will give you peace. Do not allow well-meaning people to take charge or try to bury the memories with your child.

For Angel's Going Home Service, I wrote a poem while I was still in the hospital. I gave her the godparents I had selected before her birth, before her death.

An Open Letter to My Angel

We measure life so often by its length and not by its quality or its purpose. Angel did not live out her days on earth, but lived forty short weeks in my womb. From conception to the time her precious spirit left her body, her presence was a true miracle and a blessing. To my friends who rejoiced with me throughout my pregnancy, our verse to you is:

Hebrews 13:2
"Be not careful to entertain strangers, for thereby some have entertained angels unaware."

To my Angel my verse to you is:

Ecclesiatics 3:1
To everything there is a season, and a time to
every purpose under heaven.

Thank you, Angel for our time. I shall see you again, and we shall know each other.

Love,
Your mom

(Funeral or Memorial Service)

Emotional Fusion

When Angel was delivered, it occurred to me that the stages of grief—shock, denial, blaming, anger, and finally acceptance, were not adequate. When a child is delivered stillborn or dies shortly after birth, something happens that confuses the emotions of joy and grief together. I have named this stage "emotional fusion".

This phase is a combination of that feeling a mother has (especially if this is her first child) anticipating the birth of her child, and the anguish of the unthinkable happening at the same time?

The only analogy I can think of that portrays this emotion is to imagine being a little girl, anticipating Christmas. Presents are wrapped with pretty bows and placed under the Christmas tree. Every so often you pick up a package and feel the size of the gift, shake it, and listen to the contents rattle. In your mind's eye, you have imagined what's inside the box, and it's what you always wanted.

Now imagine that on Christmas morning you are awakened to find that you house is on fire and everything you wanted and hoped for has been reduced to dust and ashes.

Notes:
(Stages of grief-shock, denial, blaming, anger and acceptance.)

One Month Anniversary

Second Month Anniversary

Third Month Anniversary

Fourth Month anniversary

Fifth Month Anniversary

Sixth Month anniversary

Seventh Month Anniversary

Eighth Month Anniversary

Ninth Month Anniversary

Eleventh Month Anniversary

One-year anniversary. (You have made it through one of the most difficult years of your life. Be kind to yourself. Plan for the day, even if your plan is to stay in bed with the covers pulled over your head. Whatever you do, it is right for you!)

Notes\Plans\Remembrance:

Anger Is the Hardest Stage

No stages of grief were separate; they all overlapped for me. Just as I thought I was finished with one stage, it would creep back.

The hardest stage for me was anger. It was torture every time I heard someone say "It was God's will," or "God knew what He was doing."

God. My higher power was the only one I have always felt I could cling to even when no one else was around. Now I was being told that this power deliberately took my child from me. For me, my saving grace was a book by Harold S. Kushner, <u>When Bad Things</u> <u>Happen to Good People</u>. In this book Rabbi Kushner said he believed

"Fate, not God, sends us problems. God does not cause our misfortunes some are caused by bad luck, some are caused by bad people, and some are simply an inevitable consequence of our being human and being mortal living in a world of inflexible laws."

It was, and is important for me to believe God did not will Angel's death
Her death was a logical (unfortunate) consequence of complications—some medical and others man-made. God did not leave me. God did not forsake me.

How are you dealing with Anger?

Notes:

She's Leading the Way

I always felt that when I died, I would die before my children and I would light their path.

I remember at the funeral thinking how unnatural it felt, as the small container bearing my child's body was placed in the ground.
The coffin was so small, too small, and all my pain couldn't fit!

During the service I expected Angel's dad to do something to stop it from happening.

Notes:

Notes:
(Inspirational poems and quotes)

Going Home

After the service, and after all well-meaning friends and family members had consoled me, I still had to go back home—alone.

I had to face the empty crib, the baby shower gifts and those precious items that I had envisioned putting on the baby.

I begged Lisa for weeks before I returned to my apartment to remove all of Angel's clothing and take down the crib. I wanted everything to be gone, out of sight, forgotten.

Thank God, Lisa didn't follow my instructions. I don't know what I would have done if those cute little infant jeans had been given away! Picking up the baby's belongings, however, was one of the hardest, most painful tasks I had ever done. It was final, and I needed to do it myself. Indeed, it was the beginning of my healing.

My moods shifted between numbness and intense, inner pain. Some days it was difficult, if not impossible to get myself out of bed. Some days I didn't fight the bed, I just gave in to it.

Notes: (Take hard days one day at a time.)

Special Days/
Special Memories

Holidays for me took on different meanings. Mother's Day became the day I visited Angel's grave. I slept completely through Christmas, and I marked what was to be Angel's first birthday with a pink carnation on my lapel.

I discovered that the more I tried to ignore important anniversary dates, the more they depressed me. However, the more I acknowledged the "special day" and planned for it, the more inner peace I achieved.

There are many beautiful ways to remember a child's brief life, many ways to come to a point of resolution, so you can let go and find personal peace.

Memorials are just the expression of memories. Also, they were ways to allow me to hold onto my role of being a mother, a role that is/was hard to give up)

I came up with projects, such as designing Angel's grave-stone (a simple white marble stone with gold lettering), or shopping for just the right flower to plant at her graveside.

A girlfriend symbolically expressed the release of her seven-year-old son's spirit by gathering with her husband, children, friends and relatives at her son's favorite playground and sending balloons with messages in them into the air. She also planted a seven-year-old evergreen during the Christmas season. Later she remarked to me, "I laughed when I saw this small skimpy tree next to the other ones. It reminded me of him"

As each child is a unique expression of our love, so too are the individual, creative, and unique ways we can pay tribute to that life, such as sending a donation in your child's name to a children's

Organization, writing a poem, a song, a book, having the child's birthstone set in a ring or necklace, or just taking time alone at the seashore, or volunteering to work a grief hotline. A living tribute to you child will never die!

<u>Notes and Plans for a Tribute:</u>
(You may not be ready to do anything for a year or more. Do not push it. Be kind to yourself)

A Separate Peace

Going through pregnancy as a single woman was a lonely experience for me. Going through the death of my child alone was devastating.

It was my inner voice I heard many nights that calmed me back to sleep when I was awakened by nightmare. It was my arms many times that wrapped around me and held me together.

I dealt with my pain separately and in doing so found strength I didn't know I had, a separate, deeper peace.

Notes:
(Lonely days)

Getting to Acceptance

Everyone must find his or her own way to the light of acceptance at the end of that long tunnel of grief. For me it was a combination of factors: a journal I kept to write letters to Angel, contact with members of Compassionate Friends, participation in the Share support group, and therapy.

However, the one single event that would guide me through this stage was a dream, later interpreted by my therapist, Lillian Miller.

In the dream, I was sitting in an apartment (a combination of my first apartment, after college, and the apartment I currently lived in). My dad entered the apartment with tears streaming down his face. He said, "Don't worry about the baby any more, I saw my mother, and she said the baby is doing well, and growing nicely, (Grandma had passed away some years earlier).

Just then I turned to see Grandma sitting on my couch with a baby (about six month old) in her loving arms. She repeated what my dad had said, that the baby was doing well and growing nicely.

Then she asked me if I would like to hold her. I sat next to grandma and she placed the baby in my arms. I sat and rocked the baby and sang to her. It felt good to be able to be a mother to her. Then the baby looked up at me. She had ice blue, lifeless eyes, that frightened me, so I gave her back to grandma and thThey disappeared.

Lillian interpreted the dream, by asking what it meant to me when the baby looked up, and her eyes were blue? I replied instantly, "That she was dead."

The Interpretation

Symbols	Meaning
Grandmother	someone whom I loved and trusted on the other side
Holding my daughter	resistance to letting go of Angel
Ice-blue eyes	reality of her death
Returning baby to grandma	Realization that I could no longer hold onto her. Acceptance\resolution

There are many other symbols in this dream, but these are the four major ones. They speak of my inner belief that the spirit is eternal, that Angel has joined the other members of my family who have passed on, and that one day I'll hold her again.

I Remember Grandma

I remember how warm and safe I felt
As I rested in her arms,
Feeling her large warm breasts
As they sagged under her floral house-dress
And quiet.

When I Think of Grandma

When I think of grandma
I think first of crying,
And feel my tears burning my eyes.
I miss her sweetness.
Then I think of her place with Jesus
And envision the warm sun, resting on her face.
When I think of grandma
Dead,
I think of being exhausted after a hard day of work and how
good the Sleep will feel.

Dedicated to Mrs. Fanny Mae Barnes

Notes:
(Events, dreams or other vehicles that help lead you to acceptance)

Where Angels Go

A whisper—a prayer,
A gentle touch—a tear,

small sweet soul
Flowing into an immortal sphere,

an elusive snowflake,
perfectly made,
briefly appearing and taken away.

a hug—an embrace,
the rustler of leaves,
glimpse of a familiar face,
The peace of a gentle breeze.

A ray of sunlight—a droplet of rain,
relief from all sorrows—sojourn without pain.

To know—only
Love,
Joy,
Laughter
And
Play

To frolic with children
who have all passed this way?
that's where Angels go

Written by Melissa—an Angel's mom

Personal Information

(Counselors \ therapists \ helping professionals)professionals)

Name:
Business telephone number:
Business location:
24-hour telephone number:
E-mail address:

Name:
Business telephone number:
Business location:
24-hour telephone number:
E-mail address:

Name:
Business telephone number:
Business location:
24-Hour telephone number:
E-mail address:

Name:
Business telephone number:
Business location:
24-hour telephone number:
E-mail address:

Support Groups\Hotline numbers

Contact person:
Telephone number:
Location:
24-hour telephone number:
E-mail address:

Contact person:
Telephone number:
Location:
24-hour telephone number:
E-mail address:

Contact person:
Telephone number:
Location:
24-hour telephone number:
E-mail address:

Contact person:
Telephone number:
Location:
24-hour telephone number:
E-mail address:

Contact person:
Telephone number:
Location:
24-hour telephone number:
E-mail address:

Bibliography and Credits:

Angelou, Maya; <u>Elegy,Elegy</u>, Maya Angelou: Poems; New York; Bantam Books, 1981.

Etsinger, Jean; <u>A Little Life</u>; St. Thomas, V. I. (financed in part by a grant from the Rotary Inner Wheel Club), 1988.

Johnson, Joy; <u>When Things go Wrong</u>, What To Do If Your Newborn Dies; New York, 1981.

Kubler-Ross, Elisabeth, MD; <u>On Children And Death</u>; New York; Collier Books, 1985.

Kushner, Harold S.;<u>When; When Bad Things Happen To Good People</u>; New York; Avon Publisher, 1983.

Schwiebert, Pat, and Kirk, Paul, MD; <u>When Hello Means Goodbye</u>; Oregon; PerinatalPrenatal Loss, 1985.

Westberg, Granger E.; <u>Good Grief</u>; Philadelphia; Fortress Press, 1971.

The Circle Game

In Celebration of Angel and Gabrie on what would have been Angel's fifth birthday.

The Circle Game

The circle of time, the circle of tears…
The circle of joy, the circle of fears…
Round and round it goes…
Of beginnings or endings,
Who really knows?

A segment of time—a linkage of life, the empty arms-
The empty crib,
A roomfull of toys, and full of books.
One child who would be turning five,
The other toddles mischievously toward two.

The circle of time, time circle of tears,
From spotless, pressed and grieving mommy—to
Tattered, crinkled and sometime unkempt mommy—
Marked by tiny hands.

The circle of joy, the circle of fears…
The visible join, the invisible in our circle game
Grands, great-grands, our special papa man,
Linked through our hearts—connecting our hands.

My now child/ my visible child, giggles and laughs,
Holding hands in her favorite circle game,
Singing, "all fall down!"

Round and round and round we go…
Of beginnings and endings, no one knows…

Happy Birthday to my two girls who play on
Opposite sides of the circle game.

Love, Mommy

0-595-28915-0